CONTENTS

How to Train a Sugar Mama	1
EMMANUEL SIMMS	2
DEDICATION	3
ACKNOWLEDGMENTS	4
Chapter 1: Welcome to the Sweet Side of Life	5
Chapter 2: How to Tame a Sugar Mama	10
Chapter 3: Creating a Lifestyle that Attracts Sugar Mamas	17
Chapter 4: Tips for Maintaining Independence While Dating a Sugar Mama	24
Chapter 5: Social Etiquette in Sugar Mama Relationships	32
Chapter 6: Understanding the Psychology of Sugar Mamas	40
Chapter 7: Managing Expectations in Sugar Relationships	48
Chapter 8: Exploring the Boundaries of Sugar Arrangements	55

Chapter 9: The Sweet Taste of Success	62
Chapter 10: Final Thoughts: The Sugar Rush Journey	69
ABOUT THE AUTHOR	77
Books In This Series	79

HOW TO TRAIN A SUGAR MAMA

EMMANUEL SIMMS

Copyright © 2024 Emmanuel Simms

All rights reserved.

ISBN: 9798345676325

DEDICATION

To everyone who's ever dreamed big, loved bold, and dared to live outside the box. May your heart always be as rich as your ambitions, and may you always find the sweet side of life. This one's for the go-getters, the charmers, and anyone who knows that love can sometimes come with a little extra sugar.

ACKNOWLEDGMENTS

First and foremost, a huge thank you to all the real-life sugar mamas and their sweet companions—your stories, whether whispered or shouted, inspired this journey. To my friends and family who cheered me on (and laughed with me through countless drafts), I couldn't have done this without your support and humor.

To my editor, who somehow made sense of my wild ideas, and to the readers who'll flip through these pages with an open mind and a sense of adventure—thank you for joining me on this sweet, unforgettable ride.

And finally, to those who know how to live life with a little bit of luxury, love, and laughter—you're the real MVPs. This one's for you.

CHAPTER 1: WELCOME TO THE SWEET SIDE OF LIFE

The Allure of Sugar Mamas

The allure of sugar mamas is akin to the irresistible scent of fresh-baked cookies wafting through the air—impossible to ignore and profoundly enticing. Picture this: a successful woman who's not only financially savvy but also knows exactly what she wants. She's like the rare Pokémon you've been trying to catch for years, and here you are, frantically tossing Poké Balls, hoping to impress her. The sugar mama phenomenon isn't just about the financial perks; it's about the thrill of entering a world where confidence and charisma reign supreme. After all, who wouldn't want to get swept off their feet by someone who can treat them to a lavish dinner while simultaneously offering sage life advice?

Navigating the world of sugar mamas can feel like trying to read a novel in a foreign language. The key to cracking the code lies in creating a lifestyle that attracts these fabulous women. Think of it as leveling up in a video game—your avatar needs to be dressed to impress and equipped with the right skills. This means investing time in your own ambitions, hobbies, and personal grooming. A well-groomed man with a passion for something—be it pottery, coding, or interpretive dance—will surely turn heads. Show her you're not just a pretty face; you're a multifaceted gem that shines in various lights.

While it's easy to get swept away in the glitz and glamour of dating a sugar mama, maintaining your independence is crucial. This isn't a fairy tale where you relinquish your identity in exchange for a magical ride in her luxury car. Instead, think of it as a partnership where both parties can thrive. Establishing boundaries is essential. If she's spoiling you with extravagant gifts, ensure that you're still pursuing your own goals and dreams. Independence isn't just attractive; it's a must. The last thing you want is to become a decorative piece in her life —unless, of course, you're an exceptionally well-crafted sculpture.

Social etiquette in sugar mama relationships is a dance of its own, requiring finesse and a dash of charm. You wouldn't wear flip-flops to a black-tie event, right? Similarly, understanding the unspoken rules of engagement can save you from awkward situations. For instance, don't forget that communication is key. If you find yourself feeling a bit overwhelmed by her lavish lifestyle, it's perfectly acceptable to express that. Just remember to do it with a smile and maybe a side of humor. "Honey, I love the private jet, but can we make our next date a cozy movie night in?" can go a long way in keeping the communication flowing while lightening the mood.

Lastly, understanding the psychology of sugar mamas can unlock the secrets to a fulfilling arrangement. Many sugar mamas are strong, independent women who appreciate companionship, fun, and a partner who can keep them on their toes. They're not just looking for a sugar baby; they want someone who can engage in stimulating conversation and share a few laughs along the way. Managing expectations is vital; don't just focus on the financial aspect. Instead, dive deep into the relationship dynamics and explore the boundaries of your sugar arrangement. This journey can be as thrilling as a roller coaster ride, filled with ups, downs, and unexpected twists. So buckle up and get ready for an adventure that could lead to an extraordinary relationship that's anything but ordinary.

Sweetening the Deal: What's in It for You?

When it comes to sugar mama relationships, the question often arises: what's in it for you? Picture this: you're gliding through life like a well-oiled machine, but suddenly, someone drops a sugar mama bombshell in your lap. Now, before you start daydreaming about designer shoes and luxury vacations, let's break down the sweet perks that come with this unconventional arrangement. Spoiler alert: it's not just about the cash flow; it's about leveling up your life game while keeping things playful and fun.

First off, let's talk about financial freedom. You might not be rolling in dough yet, but with a sugar mama by your side, that could change faster than you can say "Gucci." Imagine having the freedom to explore your passions, whether that's launching a podcast about the latest TikTok trends or finally taking that pottery class you've been eyeing. With your sugar mama covering those pesky bills, you can focus on crafting a life that's not just about survival, but thriving while embracing your inner artist. Who knew dating could double as a personal finance hack?

But it's not all about the greenbacks; let's not forget the emotional and social benefits. A sugar mama can be your biggest cheerleader, pushing you to chase those dreams that might have seemed out of reach. She's often experienced, savvy, and knows how to network like a pro. With her by your side, you're not just dating; you're entering a world of connections that could lead to job opportunities, collaborations, or at the very least, some killer dinner parties where you can show off your charm. Who wouldn't want to be the life of the party while simultaneously expanding their professional horizons?

Now, let's sprinkle in some independence.

Yes, you read that right. While it may seem counterintuitive, dating a sugar mama can actually help you maintain your independence. You're not just along for the ride; you're actively participating in an arrangement where both parties benefit. This means you have the chance to set your own boundaries and expectations. Want to spend your weekends binge-watching your favorite series instead of accompanying her to yet another fancy gala? Go for it! The beauty of this dynamic is that you can carve out your own space while enjoying the sweet life together.

Lastly, let's address the elephant in the room: the stigma. Society loves to label and judge, but those who dare to step outside the box often find the juiciest fruits. Embracing a sugar mama relationship allows you to break free from conventional dating norms while exploring the psychology behind these fascinating women. Understanding their motivations can help you navigate the relationship with finesse, turning potential pitfalls into opportunities for growth. In a world where everyone is trying to fit into a mold, why not find a way to be the exception that proves the rule? So, what's in it for you? A whole lot of sweetness, laughter, and a dash of adventure, that's what!

CHAPTER 2: HOW TO TAME A SUGAR MAMA

Recognizing the Sugar Mama Type

Recognizing a sugar mama type is like spotting a unicorn in a field of horses; they're rare, fabulous, and often have a penchant for glitter and extravagance. First off, sugar mamas don't just appear out of thin air; they have a distinct aura that screams confidence, ambition, and a little bit of mystery. You might notice them at upscale coffee shops, sipping artisanal lattes, or at art galleries, casually dropping the names of their latest investments. If she's wearing designer heels and can talk about cryptocurrency and the latest trends in the same breath, congratulations! You've stumbled upon a potential sugar mama.

Now, let's talk about the telltale signs that you're in the presence of a sugar mama. She's likely to have a calendar filled with networking events, charity galas, and brunches that sound fancier than a Michelin-starred restaurant. If her idea of a good time involves discussing the stock market over mimosas, she's definitely someone you want to get to know better. Sugar mamas are typically successful women who enjoy their independence but are also looking for someone to share their fabulous lifestyle with. If you can keep up with her fast-paced life and throw in a few clever jokes along the way, you may just be her perfect match.

But let's not forget the charm factor. Sugar mamas tend to appreciate wit and humor, so if you can make her laugh, you're already halfway there. They enjoy the thrill of a good conversation, especially if you can sprinkle in anecdotes about your own escapades—preferably ones that highlight your adventurous side. Be prepared to regale her with tales that not only entertain but also show that you're not just a pretty face, but someone who has dreams and ambitions of your own. After all, she's looking for a partner, not a pet.

Navigating the world of sugar mamas also means understanding their boundaries. These women are often fiercely independent, and while they enjoy a little companionship, they don't want to feel like they're babysitting. Recognize that their time is precious, and they expect you to respect that. Show that you can handle your own life while still enjoying the perks of their generosity. Independence is sexy, and if you can balance your needs with hers, you'll find yourself in a delightful arrangement that feels more like a partnership than a one-sided deal.

In the end, recognizing the sugar mama type is all about the blend of confidence, independence, and a sprinkle of humor. If you can embrace the quirks of this dynamic and approach it with an open mind and a playful spirit, you'll not only attract a sugar mama your way but also enjoy the ride. So, polish those conversational skills, don your most charming smile, and get ready to dive into a world where sugar, spice, and everything nice awaits.

The Art of Flattery: Compliments That Work

Flattery is the secret sauce in the recipe of seduction, especially when it comes to charming a sugar mama. Compliments can be a powerful tool, but wielding them requires finesse, much like trying to balance a spoon on your nose at a dinner party. The trick is to ensure your compliments land with the grace of a cat leaping onto a windowsill—smooth and effortless. So, what kind of compliments work best? Think of them as the glitter on your cupcake: a little goes a long way. A well-timed, genuine compliment about her style or intelligence can light up her day, but remember, overdoing it can make you look like you're trying too hard, which is a surefire way to earn the "friend zone" badge.

When complimenting your sugar mama, specificity is key. Generic flattery is as useful as a chocolate teapot. Instead of saying, "You look nice," try something like, "That dress brings out the sparkle in your eyes, and it's almost as if the stars aligned just for you today." This not only shows that you've paid attention but also demonstrates your appreciation for her unique flair. Women (and men, for that matter) love it when someone notices the little things—like that new haircut or the way she can whip up a five-course meal faster than you can decide what to order on a Friday night. Compliments like these not only flatter but also make her feel seen, and who doesn't want to feel like a superstar?

Now, let's not forget the art of the backhanded compliment. This is a delicate dance that can either impress or implode your relationship faster than a soufflé in a thunderstorm. A comment like, "You're surprisingly fun for someone who runs a billion-dollar business!" walks a fine line. While it can evoke a chuckle, tread carefully—too much sarcasm can make her question your intentions. The goal is to keep her laughing, not to send her running for the hills. Remember, humor is your ally here. If you can make her chuckle with a playful jab while praising her accomplishments, you're golden. Just be sure to read the room and adjust your approach based on her reaction.

Another effective strategy is to sprinkle in some flattery about her ambitions. Sugar mamas appreciate partners who recognize their drive. Compliments like, "Your work ethic is inspiring; I can't believe how you juggle your career and still have time to look this fabulous!" not only acknowledge her hustle but also subtly position you as an admirer of her success. This creates a bond over shared aspirations and admiration. Plus, it shows that you can appreciate her independence while still being the charming, supportive partner she wants. After all, who wouldn't want a cheerleader who's also a best friend?

Lastly, timing is everything. A compliment delivered at the right moment can feel like the cherry on top of an already delicious sundae. Whether it's during a casual dinner or while she's sharing her latest triumph, being attuned to when to drop that compliment can elevate your game from amateur hour to seasoned pro. So, keep your ears open and your compliments ready. When the moment strikes, throw in a clever quip or a heartfelt compliment, and watch as her eyes light up. Just remember: the right words, at the right time, can turn a casual encounter into a sweet connection that might just lead to a delightful sugar arrangement.

Navigating Her World: Interests and Hobbies

When it comes to navigating the whimsical world of your sugar mama, understanding her interests and hobbies is like finding the map to a treasure chest filled with diamonds and gourmet chocolate. Sugar mamas come with a unique set of passions that can range from the extravagant to the downright quirky. Whether she's into fine wine tasting, indulging in the latest wellness trends, or passionately advocating for endangered species of sea turtles, each interest is a gateway to deepening your connection. So, grab your metaphorical compass and get ready to chart a course through her hobbies, where the only danger is running out of conversation starters.

First things first, doing a little reconnaissance

never hurt anyone. Spend some time scrolling through her social media, and not just for those enviable vacation pics. Look for clues about what makes her tick. Is she posting about her latest pottery class? Or maybe she's sharing her epic fails in her quest to master the ukulele. This is your chance to slip into her world like a suave secret agent. Engage with her hobbies authentically. If she's all about that pottery life, why not surprise her with a trip to a studio? Nothing says "I'm invested" like showing up with clay-covered hands and a half-baked (pun intended) bowl that looks like it survived a minor earthquake.

Now, while diving into her interests is crucial, remember that you're not just a supporting character in her movie; you're the star of your own show. Maintain your independence by sharing your own hobbies and passions. Whether you're into extreme couponing or can recite the entire script of "Mean Girls," bring your quirks to the table. This dynamic keeps things spicy and prevents the dreaded "I'm here to fund your lifestyle" narrative from taking over. Your sugar mama will appreciate your individuality, and who knows? You might just inspire her to try something new—like extreme couponing. (Okay, maybe not, but a guy can dream!)

In the realm of social etiquette within sugar mama relationships, it's essential to navigate her interests with a dash of finesse. If she invites you to a fancy gala where everyone is sipping overpriced champagne and discussing the virtues of artisanal pickles, don't just stand there like a deer in headlights. Embrace the moment! Brush up on some casual conversation about her interests, or better yet, throw in a quirky anecdote about your own. The goal is to blend your worlds together seamlessly. After all, the more you know about her passions, the more you can charm her with your wit and wisdom, turning those awkward silences into laughter-filled exchanges.

Finally, managing expectations is key. Not every adventure will be a wild success; some may turn out to be downright bizarre. Maybe the pottery class ends with you covered in more clay than your masterpiece, or the wellness retreat reveals that you're allergic to kale. Embrace these mishaps as part of the journey. Laugh about them together and turn those moments into inside jokes. By understanding her interests while keeping your own flair alive, you're not just taming a sugar mama; you're crafting a relationship dynamic that's as rich and delightful as the finest chocolate truffle. In this sugary adventure, both of you will find joy in the unexpected, proving that love and laughter are the sweetest rewards.

CHAPTER 3: CREATING A LIFESTYLE THAT ATTRACTS SUGAR MAMAS

Upgrade Your Wardrobe: Fashion Faux Pas to Avoid

When it comes to attracting a sugar mama, the first thing to consider is your wardrobe. A well-curated look can be the difference between being noticed and being ignored. Let's face it, nobody wants to be the guy with the "I just rolled out of bed" aesthetic. So, ditch the sweatpants that have seen better days and those graphic tees that scream "I'm still living in college." Instead, think of your outfit as your first impression. An outfit should say, "I'm ready for brunch, not a Netflix binge." Remember, the goal is to look effortlessly put together, like you just strolled out of a fashion magazine, even if you had to Google "how to wear a blazer."

Now, let's address the elephant in the room: socks

with sandals. If you've ever considered this a fashion statement, consider this your wake-up call. This combo is not just a fashion faux pas; it's a crime against style. You want to be the man who turns heads, not one who causes double-takes followed by horrified gasps. Opt for some sleek loafers or stylish sneakers. If you can't decide between comfort and style, remember that looking good is part of the comfort. So, invest in shoes that don't make you look like a dad on vacation unless that is the vibe you're going for—then, by all means, embrace it.

As you navigate the world of fashion, be mindful of your fit. Clothes that are either too tight or too loose can easily turn you from a suave gentleman into a walking cautionary tale. If you're looking like a sausage stuffed into a casing, or swimming in fabric that could house a small family, it's time for a wardrobe intervention. Tailoring is your friend. A good fit is like a good sugar mama; it enhances your best features and makes you feel like a million bucks. So, skip the baggy shirts and overly snug pants, and find that perfect balance that says, "I'm confident, and I know what I'm doing."

Colors and patterns can be your best allies or your worst enemies. While we all love a bold statement, avoid looking like you got dressed in the dark or raided a circus wardrobe. Bright colors can be fun, but if you look like a walking highlighter, it might be time to tone it down. Earthy tones and classic patterns can elevate your look without making you feel like you're auditioning for a role in a bad rom-com. And while we're on the topic, let's leave the novelty prints for pajama parties. You're not just trying to impress your sugar mama; you want to make her think, "Wow, he has a personality that matches his style."

Lastly, let's talk accessories—less is more, but more can be a big mistake. A classic watch is timeless, while too many bracelets can make you look like you're auditioning for a pirate movie. Keep it simple: a nice watch, maybe a subtle necklace, and you're good to go. Remember, your accessories should enhance your look, not overshadow it. The goal is to create an ensemble that makes your sugar mama think, "He's got style and knows how to take care of himself." With these tips in your back pocket, you're ready to tackle the world of sugar mamas with confidence, charm, and a wardrobe that doesn't scream "fashion faux pas."

The Perfect Social Media Profile: Filters and All

A perfect social media profile is your digital calling card, and when it comes to attracting a sugar mama, it's all about the sweet filters and even sweeter vibes. First off, let's talk aesthetics. Your profile picture should scream "I'm fun, but I also enjoy a good brunch." Ditch the selfies that look like you just rolled out of bed. Instead, find that one photo where you're sipping a frilly drink at a rooftop bar, preferably with a stunning view in the background. Bonus points if you're wearing sunglasses and looking mysteriously contemplative, like you're pondering the meaning of life or, at the very least, what to order for dessert.

Now, let's sprinkle in some personality. Your bio should be a delicious mix of charm and wit. Think of it like a cocktail: a splash of humor, a dash of ambition, and a hint of mystery. You want to intrigue but not confuse. Something like, "Aspiring donut connoisseur, part-time poet, and full-time charmer—let's explore the world one sugar-filled adventure at a time!" This gives off just enough "I've got a personality" vibes while leaving them wanting to know what kind of donuts you're into. After all, who can resist a guy who knows his pastries?

Next, let's dive into the content you're sharing. Your feed should be a well-curated gallery of your life that showcases your interests and lifestyle without making it look like you're trying too hard. Post pictures of your hobbies—like that time you tried to become an amateur chef and almost set the kitchen on fire. Share a few snapshots from your travels, preferably with you looking effortlessly dapper. Remember, it's not just about what you post, but how you frame it—every photo should tell a story that hints at the fabulous life you lead, one that a sugar mama would want to be a part of.

Engagement is key, my friend. When you're not busy curating your profile, be a social butterfly in the comments section. Show genuine interest in others' posts, sprinkle in compliments, and don't shy away from a little flirtation when the moment calls for it. This not only builds rapport but also showcases your social skills, proving you're not just a pretty face but a delightful conversationalist. Think of it as practice for the real-life interactions you'll have with potential sugar mamas—because let's be real, charm is your best accessory.

Finally, remember to keep it real. While we all love a good filter, authenticity is the cherry on top of your social media sundae. Share your failures along with your successes. It's okay to admit that your cooking skills are still a work in progress. This balance of humor and honesty will not only make your profile relatable but also attract a sugar mama who appreciates depth and character. After all, in the world of sugar relationships, it's not just about the sweet life—it's about finding someone who enjoys the journey with you, even when it's a little messy.

Cultivating Interests: From Wine Tasting to Yoga

Cultivating interests is like seasoning a dish; too much of one flavor can ruin the whole thing. If you're trying to attract a sugar mama, you need to sprinkle in a variety of tastes that appeal to her refined palate. Wine tasting, for instance, is not just about sipping fermented grapes. It's an art form, a science, and let's be honest, a great excuse to drink without judgment. So, why not enroll in a local wine-tasting class? You'll learn to swirl, sniff, and sip while casually dropping knowledge bombs about tannins and terroirs, impressing her with your newfound sophistication. Bonus points if you can pair the right wine with her favorite cheese—

nothing says "I'm relationship material" quite like a well-matched brie.

Now, let's talk yoga. You might be thinking, "But I can barely touch my toes!" Fear not, because yoga is about more than just flexibility; it's about zen vibes and deep breathing. Plus, if you can master the downward dog without toppling over, you'll earn serious brownie points. Imagine her watching you gracefully transition from one pose to another while you're silently praying that no one sees you struggling to get back up. And don't forget about the post-class smoothie date! Nothing screams "I'm in touch with my spiritual side" like sipping a green concoction made from kale and the tears of your enemies.

Dabbling in these interests offers a two-for-one deal: you get to flaunt your new skills while discovering more about yourself. As you attend those wine-tasting events, you might find your palate evolving, or at least learn to fake it until you make it. Meanwhile, yoga will help you strike that delicate balance between being chill and being charming, essential ingredients in the sugar mama attraction recipe. Plus, if you ever find yourself in a "Who wears it better?" contest at the yoga studio, you'll be ready to whip out your best pose.

But remember, while cultivating interests, it's crucial to maintain your independence. You're not just a sidekick in her extravagant life; you're the co-star. Balance is key here. Engage in activities that make you feel like the best version of yourself, not just a trophy on her arm. So, if her idea of a good time is sipping Chardonnay while discussing the latest art exhibit, you should also be hitting the gym or playing video games with your buddies. A sugar mama will appreciate a partner who can hold their own and isn't afraid of the occasional night out without her.

In the end, cultivating interests is more than just a strategy; it's about layering your personality like a fine dessert—sweet, complex, and utterly irresistible. So fill your life with diverse activities that spark joy and intrigue, whether it's tasting wines or mastering yoga poses. Approach these experiences with humor and authenticity, and you'll not only attract a sugar mama but also create a lifestyle that's genuinely fulfilling. After all, the best relationships are built on mutual interests, laughter, and the occasional shared bottle of wine—preferably one you can pronounce without sounding like you just came from a high school French class.

CHAPTER 4: TIPS FOR MAINTAINING INDEPENDENCE WHILE DATING A SUGAR MAMA

Balancing Act: Your Life vs. Her Lifestyle

Navigating the waters of a sugar relationship can feel like tightrope walking over a pit of alligators —thrilling, a little dangerous, and requiring a good sense of balance. When you find yourself on the receiving end of a sugar mama's attention, you might think it's all roses and champagne brunches. But hold onto your avocado toast, because maintaining your own lifestyle while accommodating hers can be a challenge. You're not just a charming accessory to her fabulous life; you need to ensure that your identity and aspirations don't get drowned in her luxurious whirlpool.

First off, let's address the elephant in the room (or in this case, the designer handbag). The allure of a sugar mama's world is undeniable, filled with luxury experiences and lavish outings that can make even the most mundane Tuesday feel like a VIP event. However, amidst the glitz and glam, it's crucial to remember that your life goals and hobbies matter too. It's all about finding that sweet spot where her lifestyle doesn't overshadow your own. So, while she's planning her next spa day, don't forget to pencil in some time for your own passions —whether that's hitting the gym, pursuing a side hustle, or binge-watching your favorite series in comfy sweatpants.

Now, let's talk about the art of compromise, which is basically the relationship equivalent of sharing your fries—painful but necessary. Sugar mamas often have jam-packed schedules filled with brunch dates and charity galas, but that doesn't mean you should become a mere plus-one to her fabulous life. It's all about creating a balance where you can join her in her adventures while also carving out space for your own interests. Suggest fun activities that both of you can enjoy together, like a cooking class or a quirky art exhibit, while also keeping some evenings for your own social escapades. Just because you're dating a sugar mama doesn't mean you should put your life on hold— after all, you don't want to lose your flavor in her sugary world.

Communication is key here, and if you think it's easy, you might want to rethink that. Talking about your needs and desires can feel like walking a minefield, especially when she's used to being the one who calls the shots. But don't shy away from these conversations! Approach them with humor and honesty. Maybe start with a playful jab about how "this sugar mama needs to learn some sugar daddy etiquette" or something equally cheeky. It's all about finding the right words to express your need for balance while keeping the mood light. This way, both of you can feel heard, and you can work together to create a relationship that respects both your lifestyles.

Lastly, remember that being in a relationship with a sugar mama doesn't mean you have to relinquish your independence. In fact, the most successful sugar arrangements are those where both partners maintain a sense of self. Embrace your quirks, continue to grow your network, and cultivate your own friendships outside of her circle. This not only keeps you grounded but adds an element of intrigue to your relationship. When you have your own pursuits and passions, you become more than just a trophy partner; you become an equal player in this sweet, unconventional game of love. So go on, find that balance, and enjoy the ride—because in the end, it's all about crafting a life that's not just sugar-coated but genuinely fulfilling.

Keeping Your Finances in Check

When it comes to dating a sugar mama, maintaining your finances is like trying to balance a spoon on your nose while riding a unicycle—tricky but totally doable with a little practice. First things first, you've got to have a budget that would make even the most frugal accountant nod in approval. Let's face it, while your sugar mama might be rolling in dough, you don't want to be the one asking her for a loan to cover your latest gaming binge or that artisanal avocado toast habit you just can't quit. Set boundaries on your spending, and remember: just because she dangles a designer handbag in front of you doesn't mean you should go all-in.

Next, keep track of your expenses like you're a contestant on a cooking show, and the prize is financial independence. Use apps to monitor your spending—trust me, they're more reliable than your memory after a night out. You might think a couple of cocktails won't hurt your wallet, but suddenly you're staring at a tab that could feed a small village. Keep it real with your finances, and you might just impress her with your savvy budget skills. Who knew that being responsible could be so attractive?

Independence is key, so make sure you're not living in a financial fairy tale where your sugar mama pays for everything. While it's tempting to let her pick up the tab at every fancy restaurant, you don't want to lose your identity as an independent adult. Contribute where you can—whether it's planning low-cost dates that show off your creativity or pitching in for the occasional dinner. Remember, a sugar mama is looking for a partner, not a financial leech. Keep the romance alive by being proactive and showing that you can hold your own in both love and life.

Now, let's talk about those awkward yet essential

conversations about finances. Just like you wouldn't want to discuss your exes over a romantic dinner, you also don't want to bury your head in the sand when it comes to money matters. Set up a time to chat about expectations, budgets, and what you both bring to the sugar table. Don't let the sugar rush cloud your judgment; being upfront will save you a lot of headaches and potential misunderstandings down the line. After all, transparency is the secret ingredient to a lasting relationship.

Lastly, remember to keep your financial goals in check. Just because you're dating a sugar mama doesn't mean you should abandon your dreams of financial stability. Use this opportunity to learn from her financial habits and perhaps even tap into her network for career growth. A sugar mama can be an incredible mentor if you play your cards right. So, keep your eyes on the prize—whether that's a new business venture, a side hustle, or an epic vacation fund—and don't forget to enjoy the ride. After all, a sugar relationship can be sweet, but it's your responsibility to keep it from turning into a sugar crash.

Pursuing Your Own Passions

Pursuing your own passions is like finding the secret sauce that makes you irresistible to sugar mamas. Imagine walking into a room, exuding the confidence of someone who just devoured a double scoop of their favorite ice cream, and the aroma of freshly baked cookies wafting through the air. When you actively engage in what you love, it not only fills your life with joy but also makes you a magnet for those fabulous sugar mamas who have an eye for ambition. Whether it's perfecting your culinary skills or mastering the art of interpretive dance, let your passions shine, and soon you'll find sugar mamas lining up to share their sweet treats with you.

Now, let's talk about the importance of authenticity. Sugar mamas can spot a poser faster than a cat can knock a glass off a table. If you're pretending to be an avid rock climber just to impress her, you'll end up scaling the walls of your own embarrassment. Instead, embrace your quirks and interests, however niche they may be. Whether you're into collecting rare action figures or have an obsession with knitting, owning your passions will not only make you more relatable but also create interesting conversation starters. Who wouldn't want to date someone who can regale them with tales of their epic battles at the local comic book store?

Balancing your passions with the sugar mama lifestyle can feel like walking a tightrope while juggling flaming swords. But fear not! One of the best ways to maintain your independence is to set boundaries that allow you to pursue your interests without losing sight of your relationship. Communicate clearly with your sugar mama about your passion projects, whether it's an art class or a podcast about obscure 90s sitcoms. When she sees you dedicated to your craft, she'll appreciate your drive, and who knows? She might even want to support you by being your number one fan or, better yet, your podcast's first guest!

Now, let's sprinkle in some humor about the expectations that come with dating a sugar mama. It's crucial to manage these expectations like you would a delicate soufflé—too much pressure, and it'll collapse. Understand that while she may be financially generous, she's not your personal ATM. Instead, focus on creating experiences that allow both of you to enjoy each other's company without hefty price tags. Go for a walk in the park, have a picnic, or even host a game night with snacks you've whipped up. Trust me, nothing says romance like a well-played game of Monopoly, especially when someone lands on Boardwalk!

Lastly, never underestimate the power of social media in pursuing your passions. In this digital age, sharing your journey can attract attention not just from potential sugar mamas but also from like-minded individuals who appreciate your unique flair. Post about your latest culinary creation or your weekend hiking adventure with the hashtag #SugarMamaApproved. This not only showcases your personality but also sets the stage for potential matches. Plus, you might just go viral for that time you tried to flip a pancake and ended up creating a pancake Picasso. Pursuing your passions isn't just about self-fulfillment; it's about crafting a life that's as sweet as the sugar mamas you hope to attract. So get out there, dive into what you love, and watch your social circle—and romantic prospects—expand like a perfectly risen soufflé!

CHAPTER 5: SOCIAL ETIQUETTE IN SUGAR MAMA RELATIONSHIPS

The Dos and Don'ts of Introductions

When it comes to making a memorable introduction, there are a few golden rules to follow, and a few faux pas to avoid. First off, the dos: always lead with confidence. Strut into the room like you've just won the lottery—because in a way, you have; you're about to meet someone who might just upgrade your lifestyle. A firm handshake or a cheeky wink can set the tone for a delightful encounter. And don't forget to sprinkle in a bit of humor. A well-placed joke can break the ice faster than a well-aimed snowball at a winter party. Just remember, jokes about your ex or that time you accidentally wore your shirt inside out to a big meeting? Probably best left for another time.

Now, onto the don'ts. The biggest no-no in introductions is being too eager. Channel your inner cool cat—no one wants to feel like they just stumbled into a high-pressure sales pitch. If you come on too strong, it's not going to feel like a sugar mama relationship; it'll feel more like a sugar shock. Keep it casual. A relaxed vibe is key, as if you're both just two friends meeting for a cup of coffee rather than a job interview where the salary is your life's ambition. And for the love of all that is sweet, avoid talking about your bank balance or your "future plans" at this stage. Let's keep it light, shall we?

Another essential is to be genuinely interested. Ask questions, listen intently, and engage in the conversation like you're at a lively dinner party and not a high-stakes negotiation. This is where you can work your charm, showing that you're not just eyeing the sugar mama lifestyle, but you're also a catch in your own right. Throw in a compliment here and there—just keep it classy. Too many compliments can come off as insincere, turning your sweet approach into a sticky situation. Remember, it's about building rapport, not writing an ode.

On the flip side, don't wing it. Sure, spontaneity can be charming, but showing up unprepared can lead to awkward silences that feel longer than a Monday morning. Have a few go-to topics in mind —trending shows, travel experiences, or even the latest social media crazes. This isn't just small talk; it's your chance to showcase your personality while subtly hinting at your adventurous spirit and zest for life. Just stay away from anything too heavy or political unless you want the vibe to go from sugar rush to sour patch in under a minute.

Lastly, remember that introductions set the stage for everything that comes next. Don't be afraid to be yourself, but keep an eye on the vibe. If your sugar mama seems to enjoy a bit of banter, go for it. If she's more reserved, tone down the antics. The goal is to create a connection, not to scare her off with your extensive collection of cat memes or your fascination with conspiracy theories. By balancing charm and authenticity, you'll find that the right introductions can lead to the kind of sweet relationship you've been dreaming of—one filled with laughter, adventure, and maybe a few lavish dinners.

Handling Awkward Situations Gracefully

Awkward situations are like the uninvited guests at a party; they show up when you least expect it and often leave you wondering how to gracefully escort them out without spilling your drink. In the world of sugar mamas, where the dynamics can be as unpredictable as a cat on a hot tin roof, knowing how to navigate these moments can turn potential disaster into delightful banter. Picture this: you're on a date, and suddenly, your sugar mama brings up her ex who she claims is "still a good friend." Cue the eye roll and the mental preparation for a conversation that may require a degree in emotional gymnastics. The trick here is to embrace the awkwardness with humor. Throw in a light-hearted comment about how you'd rather discuss her favorite flavor of ice cream than her past romances, and watch the tension melt away.

When faced with an awkward silence, you might feel like a deer caught in headlights, unsure whether to flee or freeze. Instead of succumbing to the pressure, channel your inner comedian. Silence doesn't have to be deafening; it can be an opportunity for a spontaneous game! Challenge her to a round of "Two Truths and a Lie," where you both share ridiculous facts about yourselves. This not only lightens the mood but also helps you learn more about each other in a fun and engaging way. Remember, the goal is to transform the cringe into a chuckle, making the moment memorable for all the right reasons.

Another common hiccup arises when discussing finances. Nothing says awkward like that moment when you accidentally mention your student loans while your sugar mama casually flaunts her designer handbag. Instead of cringing, lean into the humor of the disparity. "Well, I suppose my student loans are my version of designer accessories!" is a great way to ease the tension. After all, sugar mamas appreciate a sense of humor and confidence even more than a perfectly polished credit score. This playful approach can also lead to deeper discussions about financial goals and support systems, turning a potentially uncomfortable topic into a bonding experience.

Social gatherings can often feel like navigating a minefield of expectations, especially when introducing your sugar mama to your friends. You might worry about their judgment or, worse, the dreaded "What do you do for a living?" question. Instead of sweating bullets, arm yourself with a witty one-liner to deflect any probing questions. "She's my financial advisor—just with a much better sense of style!" This not only lightens the mood but allows you to steer conversations away from specifics while keeping the focus on the fun. Plus, who doesn't want to be the life of the party, even if your sugar mama is the one with the real financial wisdom?

Finally, if an awkward moment slips through the cracks, don't panic; it's all part of the adventure. Whether it's a miscommunication about plans or an unintended faux pas, the key is to embrace the unpredictability of sugar relationships with a smile. Acknowledge the slip-up with a wink and a playful remark, and you'll find that laughter can smooth over even the most awkward situations. After all, the essence of dating a sugar mama is about enjoying the journey, embracing the quirks, and creating a story worth telling—preferably one that's sprinkled with humor and topped with a cherry of charm.

Navigating Friends and Family: The Sugar Mama Approval

Navigating the intricate web of friendships and family dynamics while courting a sugar mama can feel like walking a tightrope over a pit of alligators with a blindfold on. One wrong move and you could find yourself in a whirlwind of unsolicited advice, awkward questions, and, heaven forbid, judgmental looks that could curdle milk. First off, prepare yourself for the inevitable family gathering where questions about your relationship will rain down like confetti at a parade. "What does she do for a living?" "Is she really that much older than you?" and the classic, "Are you sure this isn't just a phase?" Remember, humor is your best ally here; a well-timed quip about being a "professional sugar connoisseur" can lighten the mood faster than you can say "sugar rush."

Your friends will also have their opinions, often delivered with the confidence of a thousand Instagram influencers. They may marvel at your sugar mama situation, but deep down, they're probably just a tad jelly that you're living the high life while they're stuck swiping through dating apps like they're playing a game of Tinder roulette. Use this to your advantage! When your buddies start hinting about your "unconventional" relationship, lean into it with a playful swagger. Create a faux "Sugar Mama Fan Club" where they can join for exclusive gossip and "how-to" tips on attracting their own sugar mamas. The more fun you have with it, the less they'll focus on the perceived weirdness of your relationship.

Now, when it comes to family, we all know the classic "you can't choose your relatives" dilemma. If your sugar mama has a few years, or decades, on you, brace yourself for the inevitable family intervention where everyone will passionately express their opinions, like you just announced you're running for president. To ease the tension, consider introducing her as your "life coach" or "financial planner." It's the perfect way to keep the questions at bay while subtly hinting that you're thriving under her mentorship. Plus, it leaves them with more questions than answers, and who doesn't love a good mystery?

Handling criticism gracefully is an art form, and dealing with the skeptics in your life requires a blend of charm and wit. If Aunt Edna raises an eyebrow at your sugar mama arrangements, toss out a cheeky line about how you're just "in it for the dessert" or "testing the waters of age diversity." This can deflect her concerns and spark laughter, transforming the atmosphere from judgmental to jovial. Remember, the goal isn't to convince them but to keep the peace while enjoying your sugar-filled escapades. As you navigate this social minefield, keep in mind that love is love, even if it comes with a side of financial support and a few extra years.

Finally, always remind yourself that your happiness is what matters most, and if that means dating a fabulous sugar mama who treats you like royalty, then so be it! The opinions of friends and family might sting initially, but they won't matter if you're living your best life. Establish boundaries early on, both with your sugar mama and your loved ones. Share just enough to keep them satisfied without giving away the keys to your castle. After all, this is your sugar journey, and you're the one steering the ship. So, whether you're sipping on champagne at a rooftop bar or enjoying a cozy night in, just remember to keep your chin up, your laughter loud, and your heart open – because navigating this sugar-coated adventure is all about making it your own.

CHAPTER 6: UNDERSTANDING THE PSYCHOLOGY OF SUGAR MAMAS

What Drives a Sugar Mama?

What drives a sugar mama? If you've ever wondered what fuels these fabulous women who are out here redefining the rules of dating and relationships, you're in for a treat. Imagine a blend of independence, confidence, and a sprinkle of sass. Sugar mamas, often in their prime, are typically driven by a desire for companionship that transcends the traditional norms. Maybe they've climbed the corporate ladder, conquered their careers, or simply want to have fun without the drama of conventional dating. The last thing they need is a partner who clings to them like a toddler in a candy store; they're looking for someone who can keep up with their fabulous lifestyle while adding a little spice to their already sweet existence.

Now, let's not forget the allure of freedom. Sugar mamas often appreciate the art of living life on their own terms. They've likely spent years navigating the rigmarole of relationships that come with baggage heavier than a suitcase on a budget airline. What they want is someone who can be a charming companion, not a second job. This mentality fosters a dynamic that embraces adventure, spontaneity, and, let's be honest, a touch of luxury. Who wouldn't want to sip cocktails on a beach in Bali while someone else handles the rent? It's a win-win situation where both parties can find enjoyment—just as long as you remember not to order the most expensive thing on the menu right off the bat.

But wait, there's also the psychological aspect at play. Sugar mamas often thrive on the fulfillment that comes from nurturing and guiding someone younger or less experienced. It's like being a life coach but with a few more perks—think lavish dinners, travel, and maybe even a cute little apartment in the city. For some sugar mamas, their financial prowess allows them to explore relationships that bring excitement and new perspectives, all while mentoring someone who reminds them of their younger selves. The key here is to strike a balance; being the mentee means you get to learn a thing or two while indulging in the sweet life. Just remember: don't forget to bring your A-game when it comes to charm and conversation.

Maintaining independence is another driving force behind sugar mamas. They've worked hard for their success and prefer a partner who respects that. Nobody wants a co-pilot who's trying to take the controls. This means that while they may enjoy the company of a younger partner, they don't want to be tied down by conventional expectations. They're looking for someone who can stand on their own two feet while still enjoying the perks of being in a sugar relationship. The best part? You can be your own fabulous self while enjoying the benefits of a partnership that thrives on mutual respect and excitement.

Ultimately, what drives a sugar mama is a cocktail of independence, adventure, and a touch of mentorship. They want to enjoy life to the fullest while sharing experiences with someone who can appreciate their world without trying to redefine it. So, if you're looking to attract a sugar mama, focus on being a charming companion who values your own independence while embracing the unique dynamics of this nontraditional relationship. After all, it's all about finding that perfect balance between sugar and spice.

The Power Dynamics of Sugar Relationships

The world of sugar relationships is a delightful mix of power plays and playful banter, where the dynamics are as sweet as the treats themselves. Picture this: you're charmingly navigating the relationship with your sugar mama, who's got the financial prowess to fund your lifestyle, while you bring the charisma and wit to keep her entertained. It's a classic case of "You scratch my back, and I'll let you lounge on my yacht." The key here is to understand that power in a sugar relationship isn't just about who has the cash—it's also about who has the charm, the humor, and the ability to keep things light. So, if you're looking to tame a sugar mama, it's time to wield your wit like a sword, ready to parry and thrust your way through the delightful intricacies of this arrangement.

Understanding the power dynamics at play is crucial, and it often starts with setting the right tone. You're not just another guy hoping to snag a rich partner; you're the protagonist in an urban romance novel, complete with plot twists and comedic moments. It's about striking a balance—while your sugar mama might be the one with the bank account, you're the one who can make her laugh until she spills her vintage wine. The power dynamic shifts when you realize that keeping her entertained and engaged is just as valuable as any financial contribution. After all, a relationship built solely on money can feel like a sugar rush without the candy; it's sweet but ultimately unsatisfying.

Now, let's talk about independence, a concept that often seems to vanish faster than your sugar mama's favorite dessert. It's vital to maintain your own interests and ambitions while basking in the glow of your sugar mama's generosity. This isn't just a gig where you sit back and enjoy the perks; it's a partnership where both parties should feel empowered. Think of it as being part of an elite club where you're the VIP member, and part of that membership involves bringing something unique to the table. Whether it's your interests, your aspirations, or your knack for finding the best brunch spots, remember that your individuality adds flavor to the relationship, and sugar mamas adore a well-seasoned partner.

Social etiquette plays a significant role in these arrangements, yet it can often feel like navigating a minefield while wearing roller skates. You want to ensure that you're hitting all the right notes while avoiding any awkward moments that could lead to a dramatic exit worthy of a soap opera. A simple rule of thumb is to keep the communication channels open—talk about what you both want from the relationship, set boundaries, and don't be afraid to sprinkle in a little humor. After all, nothing diffuses tension quite like a well-timed joke about the absurdity of being a modern-day gigolo. The more comfortable you are with each other, the easier it is to dance around the tricky subjects without stepping on each other's toes.

Finally, managing expectations is where the real magic happens. You might envision the perfect life filled with extravagant dinners and spontaneous weekend getaways, but it's essential to align those dreams with reality. Sugar relationships can have their ups and downs, and navigating this rollercoaster requires a healthy dose of humor and resilience. Remember, every sugar arrangement is unique, so tailor your expectations accordingly. Approach each date like an adventure with a plot twist around every corner, and keep your sense of humor intact. The real power in a sugar relationship lies in the laughter you share and the memories you create together, ensuring that even when the sugar rush fades, the sweetness of your connection remains.

Common Misconceptions: Debunking Myths

When it comes to sugar mamas, the myths swirling around them are as sweet as cotton candy but just as sticky. First off, let's tackle the big one: the idea that sugar mamas are all wealthy cougars on the prowl for a trophy. While some may fit that description, many sugar mamas are simply independent women who know what they want and aren't afraid to seek it out. They can be executives, entrepreneurs, or even creative types looking for someone to spice up their lives. So, if you think you're going to land a sugar mama by just wearing a leopard print onesie and flaunting your abs, it's time to reconsider your strategy.

Another common misconception is that sugar mamas are only interested in young, naïve men who don't know how to navigate the complexities of modern relationships. Newsflash! Many sugar mamas appreciate a partner who brings their own life experiences to the table. While youthful charm might catch their eye, what keeps their interest is a blend of humor, intelligence, and a dash of independence. So before you start practicing your best puppy dog eyes in the mirror, remember that maturity and wit can be just as attractive—if not more so—than a six-pack.

Then there's the myth that dating a sugar mama means you're signing up for a life of luxury with zero responsibilities. Sure, there's a promise of some lavish outings and indulgent gifts, but being in a sugar relationship is not an all-you-can-eat buffet without the calories. It requires effort, communication, and a healthy dose of emotional intelligence. Expecting to lounge around while your sugar mama foots the bill is a surefire way to end up back on the dating apps, swiping left in despair. You've got to bring something to the table, and that something is often your delightful personality and genuine interest.

Another delightful misconception is that sugar mamas are heartless and only want a young companion for the sake of their own amusement. In reality, these women often seek meaningful connections, even if they're unconventional. They enjoy companionship, laughter, and intimacy just like anyone else. The key here is to understand that while the arrangement may have a financial or material aspect, it doesn't mean the emotional connection is any less real. You may find that your sugar mama is more interested in sharing life's adventures than just bank accounts.

Last but not least, let's debunk the idea that sugar arrangements are inherently exploitative. This notion paints sugar mamas as predators and their partners as victims, which is a narrative that's not only oversimplified but also downright unfair. These relationships can be empowering for both parties when managed with respect and clear communication. Both sides enter into these arrangements with their eyes wide open, making it a consensual partnership rather than a transaction filled with hidden agendas. So, if you're ready to embrace this quirky lifestyle, remember that humor, mutual respect, and honesty are the ultimate ingredients for a successful sugar relationship.

CHAPTER 7: MANAGING EXPECTATIONS IN SUGAR RELATIONSHIPS

Defining the Relationship: Clarity is Key

When it comes to sugar arrangements, clarity is more than just a fancy word to toss around at cocktail parties; it's the golden ticket to a successful relationship that won't leave you feeling like you've bitten into a sour lemon. Picture this: you've just met a sugar mama who's as sweet as cotton candy but with the ferocity of a bear protecting her honey stash. Establishing clear boundaries and expectations right from the start can save you from a sticky situation later on—because let's face it, nobody wants to be the confused marshmallow in a bag of gummy bears.

First things first, let's talk labels. Are you two just hanging out, or is this a full-blown sugar arrangement? Defining the relationship isn't just a cute phrase; it's essential. This is where you need to channel your inner diplomat. You might want to ask the key questions: Are you her plus-one for events, or are you more of a "bring your own snacks" situation? Knowing where you stand is crucial because it determines everything from your date nights to whether you'll be sharing a dessert or just a Netflix password.

Now, let's not forget about the money talk. While it might feel a bit awkward—like trying to dance with two left feet—discussing financial expectations is vital. This isn't just about you getting a sugar fix; it's about mutual understanding. Is she providing a monthly allowance, or are you expected to charm her with your dazzling personality and a side of avocado toast? Setting those financial parameters will not only help keep things sweet but also prevent any sour surprises down the line.

Independence is another aspect of clarity that deserves a gold star. Sure, it's tempting to bask in the lavish lifestyle your sugar mama provides, but remember that you're still a fabulous individual with your own dreams and ambitions. Establishing that you're not just a trophy but a partner in this sugar adventure is key. Be clear about your goals, hobbies, and interests. After all, you're not just there to fill the void of her "I need someone to impress my friends" checklist; you're there to create a dynamic duo that can take on the world—while sharing dessert, of course.

In the end, the clarity conversation sets the tone for everything else. It's not just about defining the relationship; it's about crafting a partnership that thrives on mutual respect, understanding, and a sprinkle of humor. So when you sit down for that first heart-to-heart, channel your inner comedian, keep it light, and remember: the key to taming a sugar mama isn't just about knowing what she wants; it's about making sure you both know what you're getting into. After all, a little laughter can go a long way in sweetening the deal!

Communicating Needs: How to Speak Up

When it comes to communicating your needs in the world of sugar dating, think of it as a delicate dance, not a wrestling match. No one wants to engage in a verbal arm-wrestling contest with their sugar mama, but you also don't want to stand on the sidelines, twiddling your thumbs while she calls the shots. The key is to approach conversations with the grace of a gazelle and the confidence of a cat strutting through the neighborhood. Start by setting the stage: find a cozy spot where the ambiance is just right. Remember, ambiance is everything—if you're discussing your needs over a greasy burger, it might not go as smoothly as you'd hoped.

Next, it's all about choosing the right words. Think of this as crafting a fine cocktail—mix the sweet with the tart, add a splash of humor, and don't forget a garnish. Instead of saying, "I need more money," try something like, "You know, I've been daydreaming about a custom-made suit that could make me look like a million bucks. What do you think about helping me achieve that?" This way, you're not just asking for a financial boost; you're inviting her into your vision of a fabulous future. It's playful, it's engaging, and it opens the door for a conversation that feels more like a partnership than a transaction.

Timing is another secret ingredient in this recipe. No one wants to discuss needs at the wrong moment —like when she's trying to enjoy her third martini or is deep in a Netflix binge. It's all about finding those sweet spots when she's relaxed and open to dialogue. A spontaneous chat during a leisurely walk or while lounging on a sun-soaked patio can work wonders. You'd be surprised how much more receptive your sugar mama can be when she's sipping her favorite drink and is just one pun away from laughter.

Once you've broached the topic, listen actively. Communication is a two-way street, and if you're busy plotting your next snack rather than tuning into her needs, you might miss the chance to build a stronger bond. Ask her about her desires and how you can both thrive in this relationship. It's like playing catch—if you toss the ball and she doesn't catch it, you're just left standing there looking silly. Make it a fun game where both players get to score some points. Her insights might surprise you and can lead to a deeper understanding of what each of you brings to the table.

Finally, remember that being open about your needs doesn't mean you're being needy. In the realm of sugar dating, it's essential to maintain your independence while still speaking your truth. Frame your requests as enhancements to the already sweet relationship you're building together. You're not just asking for sugar; you're asking for sprinkles on top. So, keep it light, keep it fun, and watch as your relationship evolves into something that's not just about the sugar but about mutual respect and shared adventures. After all, who doesn't want to be part of a story that's as sweet as it is entertaining?

Realistic vs. Unrealistic Expectations

In the wild world of sugar relationships, managing expectations is like trying to tame a hyperactive puppy—you think you've got it under control until it suddenly decides that chasing its tail is way more fun. Realistic expectations are the leash that keeps the chaos at bay, while unrealistic ones can lead to a series of unfortunate events that would make even Lemony Snicket cringe. As you embark on this sugary adventure, remember that understanding the difference between what you hope for and what's actually feasible can save you from a world of hurt—or at least a few awkward brunches.

When you picture a sugar mama, you might dream of a glamorous woman who showers you with gifts, takes you on spontaneous trips to Paris, and knows all the best brunch spots in the city. While these fantasies are delightful, the reality is that sugar mamas are regular people too, with careers, responsibilities, and the occasional laundry day. Sure, they might love to indulge you, but expecting them to be a walking ATM or a fairy godmother is setting yourself up for disappointment. Instead, focus on building a relationship founded on mutual respect and fun. You're not just an ornament for their lifestyle; you're a partner in crime—albeit one who might occasionally need to help with the grocery shopping.

One of the biggest traps of unrealistic expectations is the notion that sugar relationships come without strings attached. Spoiler alert: they often come with a whole tangled web of strings. While the idea of living a life of luxury sounds appealing, remember that every sugar arrangement has its boundaries. Maybe your sugar mama is okay with you dating other people, or maybe she expects exclusivity. Navigating these waters requires open communication and a clear understanding of what both parties want, lest you find yourself in a relationship that feels more like a hostage situation than a sweet arrangement.

Independence is the name of the game when it comes to maintaining your identity while dating a sugar mama. It's easy to get swept up in the whirlwind of her lifestyle, but don't forget to keep your own interests and ambitions alive. Expecting your sugar mama to fulfill all your emotional needs is unrealistic, and frankly, it's a lot of pressure for her. Instead, think of her as a bonus to your already fabulous life. Cultivate your own passions, hang out with your friends, and keep pursuing your goals.

This way, you'll be the charming partner she can't help but adore, rather than a needy appendage she has to drag around.

Ultimately, the key to a successful sugar relationship lies in a balance between your dreams and reality. Embrace the adventurous spirit of the sugar lifestyle while keeping your feet firmly planted on the ground. By managing your expectations, you can enjoy the sweet moments without the bitter aftertaste of disappointment. So, grab your favorite dessert (preferably one that doesn't involve a sugar coma), settle in, and get ready to craft a life that not only attracts sugar mamas but keeps things refreshingly light and fun.

CHAPTER 8: EXPLORING THE BOUNDARIES OF SUGAR ARRANGEMENTS

Setting Boundaries: What's Acceptable?

Setting boundaries in a sugar relationship is like trying to put a leash on a wild stallion—exciting, unpredictable, and occasionally resulting in a comical disaster. So, what's acceptable in this sweet and sticky world of sugar mamas? Let's dive into the candy-coated chaos and find out how to navigate the choppy waters of expectations and autonomy without sinking the ship—or your sanity.

First and foremost, let's tackle the elephant in the room: money. In sugar arrangements, financial support is often the sweetener of the deal, but it's crucial to establish what that means for both parties. Are we talking about a monthly stipend that could fund a small country's GDP, or are we keeping it casual, like splitting the bill at brunch? Discussing finances openly can save you from awkward moments, like when your sugar mama casually asks if you'd like a new car while you're still figuring out how to pay for your daily coffee fix. Remember, clarity is key—the last thing you want is to end up with a sugar mama who thinks she's your personal ATM.

Next up, let's engage in the age-old debate of time commitment. How often do you want to see each other? Is it a Netflix-and-chill situation every other night, or are you more of a "let's catch up once a month" kind of person? Establishing time boundaries is essential, especially if you want to maintain your independence and keep your side hustle alive. After all, you can't be the next big influencer if you're too busy being someone's plus-one at a charity gala for the fifth weekend in a row. A little humor can go a long way here—try jokingly suggesting that your calendar is booked until the next lunar eclipse if you need to lighten the mood while setting your limits.

Now, let's chat about emotional boundaries, which can be as tricky as a cat on a hot tin roof. While it's tempting to let feelings flow like a bubbly soda, it's important to remember this is a sugar arrangement, not a rom-com. Be clear about your emotional availability and what you're willing to give. If your sugar mama starts dropping hints about meeting your family, it might be time to channel your inner comedian and deflect with a quip about how your family still thinks you're a professional napper. Keeping the emotional landscape light can help both of you navigate those potentially sticky conversations.

As you establish these boundaries, don't forget the essential rule of consent. It's not just about what you want; it's about what works for both of you. Open communication is vital, and humor can often break down the barriers that make these conversations feel awkward. If you need to say no to a wild weekend getaway that involves skydiving and a live performance by a 90s boy band, do it with flair. Perhaps something along the lines of, "I'd love to join, but my couch and I have a very important Netflix series to finish." Finding a way to keep it light-hearted while still being honest can turn a potentially tense moment into a shared laugh.

Finally, remember that boundaries are not walls; they're more like guidelines for a fun road trip. As you figure out what's acceptable, keep the lines of communication open and be willing to adjust as needed. Relationships evolve, and so do the dynamics of sugar arrangements. Staying flexible while respecting each other's boundaries can lead to a far sweeter experience. So, grab your map, check your snacks, and enjoy the ride—after all, the journey is just as important as the destination in this sugar-coated adventure!

Navigating Jealousy and Insecurity

Jealousy and insecurity can be like that uninvited guest at a party—awkward, uncomfortable, and completely oblivious to social cues. In the realm of sugar relationships, where the dynamics can twist and turn like a roller coaster designed by a caffeinated squirrel, these feelings can rear their heads unexpectedly. Picture this: you're at brunch with your sugar mama, sipping mimosas, and suddenly you catch a glimpse of her ex across the room. The next thing you know, you're mentally drafting a passive-aggressive tweet while inwardly grappling with the idea that he might still have her heart. Spoiler alert: he doesn't, but the mind has a way of throwing a tantrum like a toddler denied candy.

To navigate the treacherous waters of jealousy and insecurity, it's crucial to remember that relationships are not a competitive sport. Just because she's the queen bee doesn't mean you're a mere worker bee buzzing around her. Embrace your individuality and remind yourself that you bring something unique to the table—like that killer dance move you bust out at parties or your encyclopedic knowledge of obscure 90s sitcoms. Confidence is your best accessory, and it pairs nicely with a side of humor. When those green-eyed monsters come knocking, flip the script and turn jealousy into a playful inside joke between the two of you. "Hey babe, if I start wearing a tinfoil hat, just know it's because I'm convinced your ex is plotting against me!"

Communication is key, folks. It's like the Wi-Fi of relationships—without it, you'll be left buffering in the dark. If you're feeling insecure, don't hide it behind a curtain of forced smiles and awkward silences. Instead, let your sugar mama know what's going on in that beautiful mind of yours. Chances are, she's dealt with her fair share of jealousy too, and sharing your feelings can create a bond stronger than any overpriced champagne. Plus, it gives her a chance to reassure you that you're the only one who gets to call her "baby" (unless, of course, you have a puppy named Baby—then all bets are off).

Now, let's talk about the art of managing expectations. It's essential to establish the boundaries of your sugar arrangement early on. Define what's acceptable and what's a no-go. If you're both clear on the rules of engagement, you'll find that jealousy doesn't have as much room to thrive. Consider it like setting up a safe word in a particularly spicy relationship; it's all about keeping things fun while ensuring you both feel secure. Just don't use "pineapple" unless you're ready to have a very confusing conversation about fruit.

At the end of the day, jealousy and insecurity might pop up like unwanted pop-up ads on a sketchy website, but they don't have to ruin your experience. Embrace the playful banter, nurture open communication, and establish clear boundaries. Remember, sugar relationships are meant to be sweet, not sour. So the next time jealousy tries to crash your party, grab a slice of cake and remind yourself that you're the life of the gathering. After all, who wouldn't want to stick around for the guy who can make a joke out of the most awkward situations?

Knowing When to Walk Away

Knowing when to walk away from a sugar mama situation is a skill that every aspiring sugar baby should master. It's not just about dodging the emotional landmines of a relationship; it's about preserving your dignity and maintaining your self-respect. Picture this: you're at a fancy dinner, and she's gushing about her latest investment in artisanal avocado toast. If you find yourself rolling your eyes more than enjoying the caviar, it might be time to reassess your priorities. Remember, the sugar game should be sweet, not sour.

You might think that walking away means you've failed in the art of sugar dating. On the contrary! It's like knowing when to put down the dessert spoon after your third slice of cake. Sure, it felt good in the moment, but now you're clutching your stomach and contemplating a gym membership. Recognizing that you've hit your limit can save you from a future of regrettable decisions and awkward encounters. If the relationship starts to feel more like a job interview than a fun date, it's probably time to head for the exit.

But how do you know when the sugar is turning to salt? Here's a hint: if your sugar mama starts giving you unsolicited life advice on how to dress or what to eat, it's a red flag waving madly in the wind. Sure, a little guidance can be charming—like her insisting you try that new vegan place downtown. But when it morphs into a full-on makeover intervention, it might be her way of trying to mold you into her perfect specimen. Your individuality should be preserved like a fine wine, not boxed into a trendy label.

Managing expectations is key in any relationship, but especially in the sugar dynamic. If you find yourself constantly adjusting your goals to meet her whims, then it's time for a reality check. Maybe you envisioned a life filled with luxury and laughter, but instead, you're stuck planning her next spa day while your own ambitions gather dust. A sugar relationship should enhance your life, not restrict it. If you feel more like an assistant than a partner, it's a clear sign that the sugar is no longer flowing freely.

Ultimately, knowing when to walk away means understanding that your time is valuable—just like the sugar mama's. It's about striking a balance between enjoying the perks of the relationship and ensuring it aligns with your personal growth. If the sweet moments are overshadowed by stress or dissatisfaction, it's perfectly acceptable to take a step back. Life is too short for stale sugar, so keep your standards high and your heart light. After all, there's a whole world of sugar mamas out there, and the right one is just a swipe away.

CHAPTER 9: THE SWEET TASTE OF SUCCESS

Celebrating Your Wins: Small Victories Matter
In the wild world of sugar arrangements, where affection and financial support come with a sweet twist, it's easy to overlook the small wins while aiming for that grand prize of a fulfilling relationship. Let's face it, you might think that celebrating your wins means treating yourself to a lavish dinner or posting an Instagram story about your latest excursion. But hold on! Small victories, like mastering the art of texting your sugar mama without sounding desperate or finally getting her to laugh at your dad jokes, deserve their moment in the spotlight. After all, those tiny triumphs add up to create the ultimate sugar rush in your life.

Picture this: you just survived a date where you flawlessly navigated the minefield of her questions about your goals and ambitions. You didn't fumble over your words or accidentally mention your lifelong dream of becoming a professional couch potato. Instead, you charmed her with your aspirations of starting a gourmet food truck that sells only dessert tacos. That's a win, my friend! And while your friends might be out there celebrating promotions and new cars, your achievements are just as valid. So, grab a cupcake and toast to your newfound ability to keep a conversation flowing with the alluring sugar mamas of the world.

Now, let's talk about those moments when you finally get her to agree to a date that doesn't involve a three-hour discussion about her favorite reality TV shows. Maybe you suggested a fun outing that included an activity that's not just sitting in a fancy restaurant. That's an achievement worth celebrating! It shows you're not just a pretty face; you can be the guy who brings creativity and spontaneity to the relationship. The next time you hit a milestone, whether it's a successful date or a little victory in your sugar dynamic, don't hesitate to treat yourself. You deserve those celebratory moments, just like a kid deserves candy after cleaning their room—no questions asked.

Don't underestimate the power of sharing your small victories with your friends, either. You know those pals who roll their eyes at your sugar baby adventures? They'll be shocked when you recount how you managed to get her to try bungee jumping instead of just binge-watching the latest season of her favorite show. These stories become the fuel for your social circle, giving them a glimpse into the playful yet meaningful relationship you're building. Plus, who doesn't love a good laugh over the antics of dating someone who's both fabulous and financially savvy?

Finally, remember that celebrating small wins is not just about you. It's about reinforcing the bond you're building with your sugar mama. When you acknowledge the little things that make your relationship unique, you're also showing her that you value the journey you're on together. Whether it's a funny inside joke or a shared experience that made you both burst into laughter, these moments create a tapestry of memories that can sweeten any relationship. So, the next time you achieve something that feels like a small victory in your sugar adventure, don't shy away from celebrating it. Embrace it, share it, and let it add a sprinkle of joy to your sugar-filled life!

Learning from Failures: Sweet Lessons

In the sweet and sticky world of sugar relationships, every mishap can feel like a misstep in a dance you didn't even sign up for. Picture this: you're trying to impress your sugar mama with your culinary skills, only to discover that you've confused baking soda with powdered sugar. The result? A cake that looks like a science experiment gone wrong. While your intentions were good, the execution turned into a comedy of errors. But here's the kicker: those blunders are the secret sauce to success. Each failed attempt is a lesson wrapped in a sugary coating, teaching you what works and what definitely doesn't when courting your beloved benefactor.

Imagine navigating the social landscape of sugar dating like a game of Twister. One wrong move, and you're tangled up in a mess of expectations and misunderstandings. Every failed date, awkward conversation, or cringe-worthy moment is a stepping stone toward mastering the art of sugar mama relationships. Did you forget her favorite dessert during a dinner date? Use that as a launching pad to learn her tastes better—and hey, it might even lead to a fun story that gets a laugh at your next date. The key is to embrace those moments, laugh at them, and use them to refine your approach. After all, who doesn't love a partner that can turn a mishap into a memorable moment?

Now, let's talk about managing expectations. It's easy to dream big when you've got a sugar mama, but reality can be a real party pooper. Perhaps you envisioned extravagant vacations and lavish gifts, only to realize that your sugar mama prefers a quiet night in with a Netflix binge over a night out on the town. Learning to adapt and adjust your expectations is vital. Every misalignment is a chance to recalibrate and appreciate the simple joys of your arrangement. So, next time your grand plans go awry, take a moment to appreciate the cozy couch and a shared bowl of popcorn. Sometimes, the sweetest moments come from the simplest settings.

Of course, understanding the psychology of sugar mamas can feel like reading a mysterious recipe without any ingredients listed. One key takeaway from past blunders is the realization that every sugar mama has her own motivations and desires. Maybe she's looking for companionship, adventure, or just someone who can make her laugh. Each failed attempt to impress her can lead you to a deeper understanding of what she truly values. Instead of taking rejection personally, use it as a chance to ask questions, engage in conversations, and learn more about what makes her tick. This insight will help you tailor your approach, making your next attempt much more likely to hit the sweet spot.

In the end, the road to sugar relationship success is paved with laughter, unexpected twists, and a healthy dose of humility. Embracing your failures and learning from them transforms those sticky situations into golden nuggets of wisdom. So the next time you find yourself in a pickle—be it a baking disaster or a social faux pas—remember that these moments are just life's way of adding flavor to your journey. Keep your spirits high, your heart open, and your sense of humor intact, and you'll find that the lessons learned from your missteps will sweeten your future endeavors with sugar mamas.

Building a Future: Beyond the Sugar

In the quest for love—or at least a sugar rush—it's easy to get caught up in the sweetness of a sugar mama's affection. But let's not forget that building a future beyond the sugar involves more than just enjoying lavish dinners and being pampered like a prized pet. It's about crafting a lifestyle that not only attracts these generous benefactors but keeps you from becoming a mere footnote in their glittering lives. To do this, you'll want to channel your inner entrepreneur and think about what you can bring to the table that isn't just a pretty face or a charming personality. What are your passions? What unique skills do you possess? Consider yourself a brand, and like any savvy business owner, you need a vision and a mission statement that will resonate with potential sugar mamas.

Now, we all know that sugar mamas can be as complex as a six-layer cake, with layers of desires, expectations, and sometimes, a hint of drama. Understanding the psychology of a sugar mama means recognizing that independence is key. While you may be enjoying the finer things in life, it's crucial to maintain a sense of self. Show that you have ambitions that extend beyond the weekend brunches and shopping sprees. Maybe you're working on that novel that's been collecting dust or planning to start a podcast about the art of dating sugar mamas. When you present yourself as someone with goals and aspirations, you're not just a sweet treat; you're the whole dessert buffet, making you far more appealing.

But let's talk about managing expectations. In the world of sugar arrangements, it's imperative to communicate openly and humorously about what each party wants. Think of it as a negotiation where both sides need to come to the table with their own set of demands. You might want a night out at the trendiest club, while she might be looking for someone to help her pick out the perfect shade of lipstick. Finding that balance can lead to a relationship that's as delightful as a double scoop of gelato on a hot summer day. Just remember to keep the conversation light-hearted! If it feels like a business meeting, you might as well throw in some PowerPoint slides and call it a day.

Social etiquette plays a pivotal role in sugar mama relationships. Yes, you might be tempted to wear your sweatpants to a dinner date, but let's be real—first impressions matter. Think of it as dressing for the role you want to play in her life. A sprinkle of charm, a dash of humor, and a well-chosen outfit can create a recipe for success. And don't forget the little things: remembering her favorite dessert or asking about her day can go a long way in buttering her up. The key is to be genuine; no one likes a phony, even if that phony is trying to be funny.

Finally, let's explore the boundaries of sugar arrangements. The beauty of these relationships is that they can be as flexible as a contortionist at a circus. It's essential to define what works for both of you. Are you on a fixed allowance, or does she prefer to treat you to spontaneous adventures? Whatever the arrangement, make sure that the boundaries are clear and respected. This is not just about sugar; it's about respect and understanding. When you navigate these waters with a mix of humor and honesty, you'll not only attract the right sugar mama but also build a future that's sweet, fulfilling, and uniquely yours.

CHAPTER 10: FINAL THOUGHTS: THE SUGAR RUSH JOURNEY

Embracing the Unconventional

Embracing the unconventional is like walking into a trendy café where the barista has blue hair and piercings in places you never thought possible. It's about shaking off the mundane and diving headfirst into a world where traditional dating norms are tossed out the window, possibly along with some bad coffee. If you're ready to attract a sugar mama, you'll want to channel your inner rebel. Forget the cookie-cutter ideas of romance; it's time to add some sprinkles to your relationship game. After all, sugar mamas are looking for someone who stands out, not someone who blends in with the wallpaper.

Now, let's talk about the elephant in the room—or should I say the oversized unicorn in the café? Embracing the unconventional means you need to get comfortable with the unexpected. Picture this: while your buddies are swiping right in search of their next "serious girlfriend," you're out there crafting an Instagram-worthy life filled with adventures, spontaneous trips, and the occasional extravagant brunch. You're not just looking for a partner; you're curating an experience. Your social media feed should be a delightful mix of quirky quotes, delectable dishes, and snapshots of your fabulous escapades—each post a little invitation for sugar mamas to take a closer look.

But don't get too caught up in the aesthetics; there's more to it than just pretty pictures and witty captions. You'll also want to sprinkle in a dash of charm and humor. Think of your conversations as a delightful mix of banter and substance, where you can seamlessly transition from discussing the latest Netflix series to the benefits of a good skincare routine. Sugar mamas appreciate wit and intelligence, so be prepared to flex those conversational muscles. Just remember, while you're embracing the unconventional, keep an eye on your independence. It's important to create a lifestyle that doesn't just attract sugar mamas but also allows you to thrive on your own.

Another crucial aspect of this unconventional relationship dance is understanding the psychology of sugar mamas. These fabulous women often seek companionship that's refreshing and invigorating. They're not just looking for someone to shower them with attention; they want a partner who excites them, challenges them, and can keep up with their fast-paced lives. So, when you're engaging in social etiquette within this unique dynamic, remember that it's a two-way street. You can't just sit back and enjoy the ride; you've got to be an active participant, ready to navigate the twists and turns of this exhilarating journey.

Finally, let's not forget the importance of managing expectations. In the world of sugar arrangements, communication is key. Embrace the unconventional by being open and honest about what you want from the relationship. Establishing boundaries is essential, not just for your own well-being but also to ensure that both you and your sugar mama are on the same page. So, as you venture forth into this whimsical world of sugar mamas and unconventional relationships, remember to keep it light, keep it fun, and most importantly, keep it real. With the right mix of charm, humor, and a sprinkle of independence, you'll be well on your way to crafting a life that not only draws sugar mamas your way but also keeps your spirit soaring high.

The Sweetest Takeaway: Enjoy the Ride

The journey into the world of sugar mamas is akin to riding a roller coaster designed by Willy Wonka – slightly chaotic, full of surprises, and ultimately delicious if you've got a taste for adventure. The key is to strap in, keep your arms and legs inside the ride at all times, and embrace every twist and turn. You might find yourself in a whirlwind of brunches at swanky spots, extravagant shopping sprees, and the occasional spontaneous getaway to a tropical paradise. A sugar mama might just spoil you rotten, but remember, this isn't a one-way ticket to Candyland. It's all about enjoying the ride while ensuring you're not just another flavor of the month.

As exhilarating as it is to be swept off your feet by a woman who knows what she wants, it's crucial to maintain your individuality. Think of it as balancing on a tightrope while juggling cotton candy and chocolates. Sure, you love the attention and the luxurious lifestyle, but you also have your own dreams and aspirations. In this sugar-coated world, don't forget to sprinkle in a little bit of your own spice. Whether it's pursuing a passion project, hitting the gym, or binge-watching the latest Netflix series, keeping your independence is like having a secret stash of candy that's all yours.

Now, let's chat about expectations. Navigating the sugar mama scene is less about setting the bar high and more about keeping it at a comfortable level—like a good old-fashioned buffet. You want to indulge without going overboard. Be honest about what you're looking for, whether it's companionship, mentorship, or simply a taste of that sweet lifestyle. And don't forget to throw in a dash of humor to lighten the mood. After all, laughter is the best medicine, especially when your sugar mama surprises you with a last-minute trip to Paris that you weren't quite prepared for.

Social etiquette is the unsung hero of sugar relationships. It's the invisible thread that ties everything together, ensuring you don't accidentally turn a lovely dinner into a cringe-fest. Remember, you're not just there to enjoy the perks; you're also representing yourself as a charming companion. So, brush up on your table manners, practice some light banter, and be genuinely interested in her stories. This isn't just about sugar; it's about building a connection that's as sweet as the desserts you'll inevitably be indulging in together.

Finally, let's address the psychology of sugar mamas. These fabulous women are often driven by ambition, independence, and a desire for companionship that transcends traditional norms. Understanding this dynamic is essential for navigating your relationship successfully. Embrace her strengths, appreciate her independence, and, most importantly, don't underestimate her intelligence. After all, she's chosen this arrangement for a reason. So, while you're riding this exhilarating wave, keep your eyes wide open and your heart ready for whatever comes next—because with a sugar mama, the sweetest takeaway is the unforgettable ride you're on together.

Your Next Steps: Go Get That Sugar Mama!

When it comes to snagging that elusive sugar mama, the first step is to channel your inner charismatic guru. Embrace confidence like it's the hottest new trend. You don't need to be a suave James Bond or a dapper gentleman; a dash of charm and a sprinkle of humor will do the trick. Picture this: you, walking into a room full of sugar mamas, and instead of awkwardly shuffling your feet, you strut in like you own the place. Flash a cheeky smile, crack a joke about the overpriced avocado toast, and watch as hearts (and wallets) begin to open. Remember, confidence is magnetic – but don't go overboard; nobody likes a peacock that won't stop strutting.

Next, it's time to curate a lifestyle that screams "I'm the fun one!" Sugar mamas are typically independent and successful, so they want someone who can keep up with their fabulousness. Start by refining your interests and hobbies. Whether it's mastering the art of mixology or becoming the king of brunch spots, your life should be a vibrant tapestry of experiences that would make any sugar mama swoon. Post about your escapades on social media, sprinkle in some humor, and suddenly, you're not just a potential partner; you're a lifestyle upgrade. Just don't go overboard with the gym selfies unless you're trying to attract a sugar mama who's into fitness – in which case, flex away!

Now, let's talk social etiquette because navigating the sugar mama scene is like dancing on a tightrope while juggling flaming torches. You'll want to be charmingly attentive but not overly clingy. Master the art of conversation, and learn to listen as much as you speak. Ask her about her day, and when she talks about her latest business venture, don't just nod; engage! Show genuine interest and offer your own quirky insights. This isn't just about getting a free meal; it's about building a dynamic connection.

HOW TO TRAIN A SUGAR MAMA

And if you can throw in a funny anecdote about your last job interview gone wrong, you'll be golden. Just remember, if she's sharing her dreams of world domination, don't suggest a reality TV show about it unless you're ready for a wild ride.

Independence is key in any sugar arrangement. While it's tempting to bask in the glow of your sugar mama's generosity, it's crucial to maintain your own identity. Dive into your passions, keep your friendships alive, and have your own goals. This balance not only keeps you grounded but also adds to your allure. After all, a sugar mama wants someone who isn't just a trophy but a partner in crime. Plus, being a little mysterious can spark intrigue. So, while you're enjoying those lavish dinners and extravagant outings, sprinkle in some solo adventures. When she asks about your weekend, regale her with tales of your solo hike or your latest side hustle. It shows you're not just hanging around for the free rides.

Finally, let's tackle expectations. The sugar mama dynamic can be thrilling, but it's essential to establish boundaries and communicate openly. Don't let yourself get swept away in a whirlwind of luxury without discussing what you both want from this arrangement. Are you looking for casual fun, or do you hope for something deeper? Be upfront but keep it lighthearted. Think of it as setting the rules for a game of Monopoly: nobody wants to end up in jail without knowing why. So, lay down the ground rules, manage those expectations, and remember that it's all about enjoying the ride. After all, the journey to finding your sugar mama should be as sweet as the treats she might spoil you with!

ABOUT THE AUTHOR

Emmanuel Simms, author of the bestseller *How to Tame a Fck Boy: 12 Steps for Taming Your Fck Boy*, has a knack for tackling modern relationships with wit, insight, and humor. Known for his unfiltered approach and ability to turn relationship dilemmas into relatable lessons, Emmanuel dives into the quirks of love, dating, and personal growth with a fresh perspective. When he's not writing, Emmanuel dedicates his time to exploring life's complexities and encouraging readers to master their #RelationshipGoals with confidence and style.

BOOKS IN THIS SERIES
#RELATIONSHIPGOALS MASTERY

Dive into the '#RelationshipGoals Mastery' series, where modern dating meets its match. In an era where love and relationships are as complex as ever, this series serves as your compass, guiding you through the twists and turns of contemporary romance. Starting with 'How to Tame a F*ck Boy,' each edition unravels the realities of love in the digital age. Get ready to redefine your relationship goals and discover the secrets to attaining true love mastery. And keep an eye out for those easter eggs hinting at what's next!

How To Tame A F*Ck Boy : 12 Steps For Taming Your F*Ck Boy (#Relationshipgoals Mastery Book 1)

In the exhilarating dance of modern relationships, Emmanuel Simms offers a bold and candid guide to understanding, navigating, and potentially taming the enigma known colloquially as the 'Fuck Boy'.

Through "12 Steps for Taming Your Fuck Boy", Simms delves into the dynamics that make these relationships both enthralling and tumultuous. Drawing from a mix of personal anecdotes, humor, and practical advice, this book doesn't just shed light on the allure of the Fuck Boy but also offers tangible steps for those hoping to find balance in such partnerships. Whether you're caught in the throes of a whirlwind romance, seeking clarity, or just in for an entertaining read about modern love's complexities, this book is your compass. Dive in and discover a blend of humor, wisdom, and raw truths that will resonate, provoke thought, and maybe even guide you to a healthier, happier relationship dynamic.

How To Tame A F*Ck Boy - The Interactive Workbook: 12 Steps For Taming Your F*Ck Boy The Workbook (#Relationshipgoals Mastery 2)

Have you ever found yourself lost in the maze of modern dating? Caught up in the whirlwind of emotions, only to find yourself questioning the intentions of the person on the other end? Dive into this interactive workbook, a companion to the acclaimed book "How to Tame a F*ck Boy", and equip yourself with tools, exercises, and insights to navigate the tumultuous waters of relationships with confidence.

Inside This Workbook, You'll Discover:

Interactive Exercises: Dive deep into self-reflection, understanding patterns, and setting relationship goals.
Expert Advice: Grounded in Emmanuel Simms' wisdom, gleaned from personal experiences and expertise.
Journaling Sections: Pen down your thoughts, fears, desires, and breakthroughs.
Case Studies: Real-life examples showcasing the dynamics of modern relationships.
Strategies for Success: Concrete steps to establish healthy relationship boundaries.
Whether you're single, dating, or in a relationship, this workbook offers valuable lessons to improve your relationship IQ. Crafted with thought-provoking prompts and challenges, it's designed to push you out of your comfort zone, compelling you to confront and redefine your relationship expectations.

Don't just read about change. Experience it. Transform your love life one page at a time with "How to Tame a F*ck Boy - The Interactive Workbook". Perfect for those looking to delve deeper, seeking clarity, or simply wanting to be proactive in their journey towards healthier, more fulfilling relationships.

It's You: The Christmas Chronicles: A Festive Guide To Not Being A F*Ck Boy (#Relationshipgoals Mastery)

In "It's You: The Christmas Chronicles," Emmanuel Simms delivers a humorous yet insightful guide to navigating the holiday season without falling into the F*ck Boy trap. This festive edition, part of the #RelationshipGoals Mastery series, is packed with witty anecdotes, practical advice, and relatable scenarios that keep the holiday spirit alive. Whether you're single, dating, or in a complicated relationship, this book offers a unique blend of laughter and wisdom to help you avoid common holiday pitfalls. From dodgy office parties to meeting the family, Simms guides you through with his signature blend of humor and heart. Get ready to unwrap the gift of self-awareness and relationship savvy this Christmas!

Made in the USA
Columbia, SC
27 November 2024